HOW I PURCHASED 5 PROPERTIES BEFORE I BECAME A U.S. CITIZEN

THE DO'S AND DON'TS OF BUILDING AN AMERICAN REAL ESTATE EMPIRE AS A MIGRANT

MARK YU

Copyright © 2025 Mark Yu.
All rights reserved.

No part of this publication may be reproduced, distributed or transmitted in any form or by any means, including photocopying, recording or other electronic or mechanical methods, without the prior written permission of the publisher, except in the case of brief quotations, reviews and other noncommercial uses permitted by copyright law.

This manuscript represents personal experiences and opinions. Financial outcomes described are specific to the author's situation and should not be considered typical or guaranteed. Consult qualified professionals before making investment decisions.

ISBN 979-8-218-79841-3

Dedication

To my daughter, Aria: I hope you read this book when you're the right age, so you'll understand how your father's upbringing shaped the path that led to you.

To my fiancée, Irene: You've been my rock through every proverbial up and down. I love you both.

To my readers, this is my $2 million worth of real estate education that I am sharing with you.

CONTENTS

Foreword. vii

Chapter 1. From Manila Streets to American Dreams. ix

Part One: Foundations in the Philippines. 1

Chapter 2. The Weight of "Kung Hei Fat Choi" 3

Chapter 3. The Man Who Worked Until 80. 6

Chapter 4. The Education of Hustle 8

Chapter 5. The Books That Changed Everything 10

Chapter 6. My First Ventures and Failures. 13

Part Two: The American Dream Begins 17

Chapter 7. Crossing the Pacific 19

Chapter 8. My Texas Beginning. 22

Chapter 9. My Grandfather's Last Lesson 25

Part Three: My Real Estate Revelation. 27

Chapter 10. My Cleveland Discovery. 29

Chapter 11. The First Deal 32

Chapter 12. The McAllen Mistake. 35

Part Four: Scaling the Portfolio **39**

Chapter 13. The Eight-Door Gamble 41

Chapter 14. The Property Manager Education 44

Chapter 15. The Tax Disaster............................... 46

Chapter 16. The Dallas Delusion............................ 49

Part Five: Lessons from the Trenches **53**

Chapter 17. The Numbers That Matter
(And the Ones That Don't)...................... 55

Chapter 18. What They Don't Tell You About Being a Landlord 58

Chapter 19. The Psychology of Losing Money 62

Chapter 20. Why I Haven't Quit (Yet)....................... 64

Chapter 21. What I'd Do Differently........................ 68

Chapter 22. The Immigrant Advantage 71

Chapter 23. The Philippines Detour 74

Chapter 24. The Dallas Gambit and its Aftermath 76

Chapter 25. The California Experiment..................... 78

Chapter 26. The Fifth Property—Dallas Suburb, Texas 81

Chapter 27. The Trust and The Legacy...................... 85

Chapter 28. The H-1B Reality Check 87

Epilogue. Would I Do It Again? 91

Final Thoughts... 93

Appendix A. The Real Numbers 95

Appendix B. Lessons for Fellow Immigrants................. 99

Endnotes... 103

About the Author 105

FOREWORD

"Well, it says he purchased a home, a duplex, and then an eight-unit apartment complex. I'm sorry, gas is not your biggest budget item right here—you literally bought a real estate empire."

"Right, I'm just saying sometimes I think it takes money to make money."

—Ben Carlson and Michael Batnick,
Episode 267 of Animal Spirits
(YouTube), July 27, 2022.1

INTRODUCTION

From Manila Streets to American Dreams

The financial aspects mentioned in this book are not vetted by any investment, real estate, or banking professionals. Do your own due diligence. This is my story—raw, unfiltered, and filled with mistakes that cost me tens of thousands of dollars. But it's also a story of persistence, of an immigrant who arrived in America with a physical therapy degree and a dream, and who managed to build a real estate portfolio worth over $1,700,000 before even becoming a citizen.

Writing this book helped me look back at things I would otherwise have taken for granted. It reminded me of a quote about how in the moment, you don't know where you're going and the lines are blurred, but in hindsight, you can draw a line from past to present and everything just makes sense afterwards.

Just trust the process.

PART ONE: Foundations in the Philippines

CHAPTER 1

The Weight of "Kung Hei Fat Choi"

I grew up in the vibrant heart of the Philippines, cradled in a middle-class Filipino-Chinese family where life hummed with the rhythm of my grandfather's t-shirt business and the annual chant of *"Kung Hei Fat Choi"*—wishing wealth and prosperity—each Lunar New Year. Those four words weren't just a greeting in our household; they were a philosophy, a constant reminder that in our culture, financial success wasn't just personal—it was familial, generational, almost spiritual.

Our family of five shared a bustling home with my paternal grandparents in Quezon City. My younger sister, brother, and I navigated a household filled with love but stretched thin by financial uncertainty. My father, an eternal bookworm, had lined our built-in bookshelf from waist to ceiling with Feng Shui books—hundreds of them, their spines creating a colorful wallpaper of promised fortune. Yet for all his reading about attracting wealth and positioning furniture for prosperity, he never managed to find a stable job or business to anchor us.

My mother tried everything. She ventured into coin-operated karaoke machines, setting them up in impoverished neighborhoods where people would spend their last pesos for three minutes of escape. When that failed, she tried shrimp farming in Bicol. When the shrimp died, she switched to pigs. When the pigs got sick, she came home. Each failed venture left us more dependent on my grandparents' generosity.

But my grandfather—he was different. He was certainty in a world of maybes.

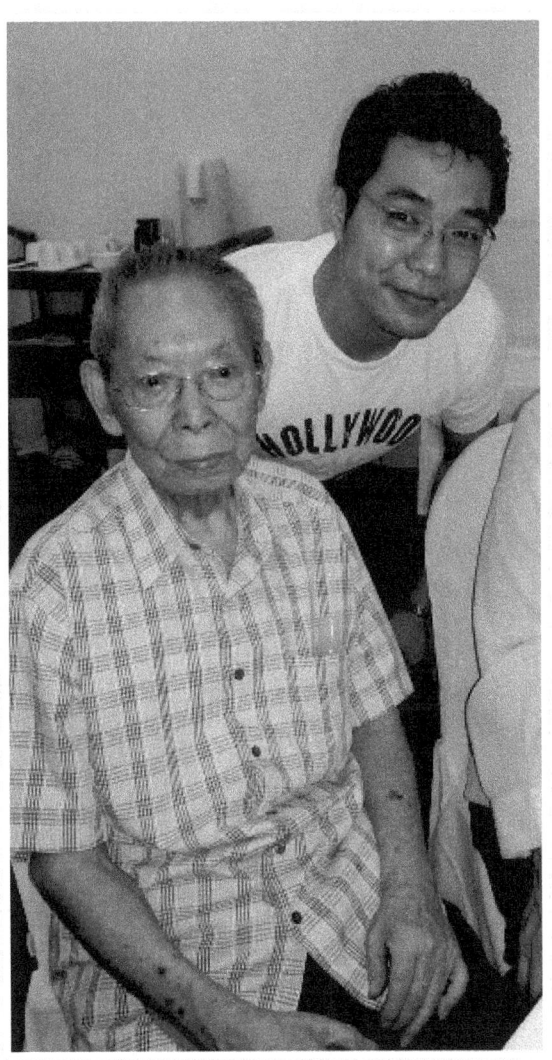

CHAPTER 2

The Man Who Worked Until 80

My grandfather arrived in the Philippines as a communist escapee from China, carrying nothing but a chemical engineering degree and an unshakeable work ethic that would shame men a quarter of his age. While others his age played mahjong in Binondo's narrow streets, he built a t-shirt printing empire one client at a time.

I remember summer weekends when I was 12, sitting in the middle seat of his three-seater Mitsubishi L300 van—the one with no air conditioning and vinyl seats that burned through your shorts in Manila heat. We'd deliver boxes of freshly printed shirts to massive factories: San Miguel's brewery, Fortune Tobacco's compounds. The security guards knew him by name. *"Ah, Mr. Ong is here!"* they'd say, waving us through gates that kept most people out.

That middle seat had no ventilation, and I'd sit there for hours, my legs burning from the engine heat below (I'm lucky I didn't become infertile from those long hours of heat exposure). But I never complained. How could I? My grandfather, in his 70s, would personally carry boxes, check quality, negotiate prices—all while wearing the same polo shirt he'd worn for 20 years, patched and re-patched by my grandmother.

> *"Money is like a river,"* he'd tell me in Hokkien, our Chinese dialect. *"It must keep flowing, or it becomes a swamp."*

When I was in high school, he arranged for me to work a summer job at my great-aunt's ball bearing company. Picture this: a factory floor with no air conditioning in Philippine summer, where the temperature regularly hits 95°F with 80% humidity. My job was to face a wall and trim ball bearing edges, one at a time, with a precision tool. I counted everything to stay sane—80 ball bearings in one particularly productive afternoon, with not a single scratch on my fingers despite the repetitive, dangerous work.

The mosquitoes at lunch were vicious. We'd sleep on wooden benches during siesta time, and I'd wake up with welts covering my arms. But I learned something crucial that summer: most people complain about their circumstances; successful people endure them while planning their escape.

CHAPTER 3

The Education of Hustle

My financial education began with survival economics. In high school, my grandfather gave me 20 to 40 pesos daily—about 50 cents—for emergencies only. A tricycle ride home cost 20 pesos. A meal at the school canteen cost 35. The math was clear: you could eat or you could ride, but not both. So, my mother packed my lunch every single day, from elementary school through high school at Grace Christian High and continuing through my exam preparation to become a licensed physical therapist. The meals were simple: rice, a piece of fried fish or a hard-boiled egg, maybe a banana, all packed in the same recycled plastic containers that were washed and rewashed until they cracked.

In college, the allowance increased to 60 pesos, but so did the expenses. The jeepney fare from our home to the University of Santo Tomas was 16 pesos each way. That left 44 pesos for everything else—photocopying, emergency food, and the occasional contribution to a group project. I learned to walk partial routes to save eight pesos, to share photocopies with classmates, and to afford a snack once in a while.

My high school friends came from different worlds. They drove new cars to school while I squeezed into packed jeepneys where you could barely breathe on occasion. They wore original Nike shoes that cost more than my family's monthly grocery budget; I wore fake Ferrari *"Farrori"* basketball shoes from Divisoria that fell apart after three months. They smelled of expensive cologne—Acqua di Gio, Clinique Happy—while I used the same bottle of local Bench cologne for two years, applying it so sparingly that the scent was more memorable than reality.

But I watched them. I studied them like they were part of my curriculum. How they talked about their parents' businesses, how casually they mentioned property investments, how they assumed wealth was reproducible, generational, inevitable. One classmate's family owned 12 rental properties around Metro Manila. Another's father was developing a car parts business. They talked about passive income like it was as natural as breathing.

That envy—raw, uncomfortable, and motivating—became my fuel.

CHAPTER 4

The Books That Changed Everything

During my third year of college, desperate to escape the allowance cycle, I lied my way into a call center job with two friends. We told them we were seeking long-term employment, knowing full well we'd leave when school resumed. The Burgundy Tower building in Makati was a gleaming tower of possibility, but getting there was hell—a nine-mile commute that took over an hour during rush hour. First, a jeepney to the MRT station (20 minutes), then standing in line for the train (15 minutes), then packed like sardines in a train car with broken air conditioning (30 minutes), then another jeepney to the building (15 minutes).

The graveyard shift paid 15,000 pesos monthly—more money than I'd ever seen. I was taking calls for American customers having internet problems, and they had no idea the person helping them was a 19-year-old Filipino who'd never owned a laptop. But that's where I learned something crucial: Americans talked about money differently. They'd casually mention their mortgage payments, their investment properties, and their retirement accounts. Money wasn't shameful or secret; it was a tool, a topic, a puzzle to solve.

After making dramatic excuses to leave when school started, I eventually returned to call center work to fund my NPTE (National Physical Therapy Examination) preparation after I finished my bachelor's degree and was unable to get a meaningful job in the profession. But between those stints, books became my real education.

It started with a rainy day in Parañaque, 1.5 hours from home. I was stranded in a 7-Eleven, holding 10 bottles of soya milk that I was supposed to sell to my teenage ACL patient at a profit. (Yes, I was side-hustling soya milk to physical therapy patients—don't judge.) The rain hammered the tin roof while I sipped from one of the bottles that I couldn't afford to drink, and I realized something had to change.

That's when I discovered Bo Sanchez's *How My Maid Became a Millionaire*. Sanchez wrote about teaching his household help to invest in the Philippine stock market, showing how even someone earning 5,000 pesos monthly could build wealth through discipline. The book revealed something shocking: in the Philippines, known for underpaying domestic workers in conditions approaching modern slavery, a maid was building a fortune while I, a college graduate, was counting pesos for jeepney fares.

I opened my first stock brokerage account the day after finishing that book.

Chinkee Tan's *For Richer, For Poorer* came next—a wake-up call disguised as financial advice. Tan, a motivational speaker who'd built his wealth from nothing, wrote about the psychology of poverty—how poor thinking keeps you poor regardless of your income. I realized I was saving money like a poor person, hoarding small amounts instead of investing for multiplication.

But the book that lit the fuse was Robert Kiyosaki's *Rich Dad Poor Dad*, which I read on overnight shifts, hiding it inside my call center training manual. Kiyosaki's words hit like lightning: *"Rich people acquire assets. The poor and middle class acquire liabilities that they think are assets."*

I started seeing everything differently. My grandfather's t-shirt business wasn't just work—it was an asset that produced cash flow. My parents' ventures weren't just failures—they were attempts to escape the employee quadrant described by Mr. Kiyosaki. The rental properties that he had mentioned weren't just houses—they were money machines.

CHAPTER 5

My First Ventures and Failures

A rmed with book knowledge and burning ambition, I made every mistake possible.

After graduating with my physical therapy (PT) degree in 2010, I couldn't find a full-time PT job. The market was saturated, and hospitals wanted experience that I didn't have. So, when a college dropout friend offered to help me get work as a real estate agent, I swallowed my pride. Weeks after taking my oath as a licensed physical therapist—a moment my family had saved for, sacrificed for, and dreamed about—I was standing in the Landmark Makati handing out flyers for condominium units that I couldn't afford to rent, much less buy.

"Affordable luxury living!" I'd say to shoppers who avoided eye contact. *"Pre-selling prices!"* Most walked past like I was invisible. But I noticed that the successful agents didn't hand out flyers. They

had clients who sought them out and networks that fed them deals. I had neither.

But the experience taught me about real estate from the ground up. I learned about pre- selling advantages, how developers priced units, why corner units cost more, and how payment schemes worked. Even as a failed agent, I was learning the language that I'd need later.

I managed to get part-time work at an orthopedic clinic in Makati, treating wealthy patients who'd hurt themselves playing golf or tennis. One patient, a Chinese-Filipino businessman, would conduct stock trades during our sessions. *"Sell my Jollibee shares,"* he'd tell his broker while I worked on his shoulder. *"Buy San Miguel at the dip."* He'd make more money in one phone call than I made in a month. I recall turning the clinic's gym TV to CNBC Asia, but the scrolling numbers and letters on the screen were confusing and hard to follow.

That's when I started cobbling together multiple income streams: home health appointments with clients in the morning (800 pesos per session), working at the clinic four to five days a week (500 pesos per day), and working weekend soccer games as a medic (500 to 1,000 pesos per day, depending on number of games). I was saving everything possible.

The call center beckoned again—it was steady money at 18,000 pesos monthly for the graveyard shift. This time I worked at a facility in Tayuman, just 30 minutes from home. I'd work from 10 PM to 7 AM, race to my morning PT appointments, crash for three hours in the afternoon, then go back to the call center. My body was breaking down, but my bank account was finally growing. And during my regular commuting in Manila, I listened to author Earl Nightingale's prerecorded talks, and one of his phrases that stuck with me was this: *"What your mind can conceive and believe, it can achieve."*[2]

Then came the investment disaster that nearly broke me.

A friend of a friend claimed to be a forex trader. He showed me screenshots of 30% monthly returns trading EUR/USD pairs. I watched my initial 20,000-peso investment grow to 26,000 in two weeks. This was it, I thought—my shortcut to wealth. I emptied my savings account— 80,000 pesos—eight months of call center slavery, every peso I'd saved by walking instead of riding, by skipping meals, and by wearing the same old rubber shoes for daily harsh commutes during that period.

Three months later, it was all gone. The *"trader"* stopped answering calls. The trading account showed zero. I then assumed that it was all just a Ponzi scheme—probably he'd been showing fake returns while gambling away our money.

I didn't eat for a few days. Not from poverty—I still had my job—but from shame and rage. How could I be so stupid? How could I fall for the exact *"hot tip"* scam that the books I read had warned against?

But failure is education with a tuition fee. I dove into real investing, studying Benjamin Graham's *The Intelligent Investor*, and watching

---

2 https://www.goodreads.com/quotes/6641738-what-the-mind-can-conceive-and-believe-it-can- achieve

Warren Buffett's practitioners use Excel and describe their stock investing styles on YouTube. I began to understand what actual investing looks like versus gambling. YouTube University, as I called it, became my MBA program.

PART TWO:
The American Dream Begins

CHAPTER 6

Crossing the Pacific

In 2012, while treating a patient at the clinic, I overheard two colleagues discussing their plans to take the NPTE. They were heading to Texas, they said. The pay was five times what we made in Manila. The words hung in the air like a door opening.

The process was complicated and expensive. First, the TOEFL (Test of English as a Foreign Language) exam (₱10,000). Then, credential evaluation through the FCCPT (Foreign Credentialing Commission on Physical Therapy) for ₱25,000. Then, the actual NPTE, which could only be taken on U.S. territory (₱25,000 plus travel). All of these fees while paying for a review center (₱30,000) and maintaining my living expenses.

I went into overdrive. I wanted to be able to afford to join my colleagues in Texas. I'd start with the graveyard shift at the call center from 10 PM to 7 AM. Then, I'd head straight to review classes at St. Louis Review Center in Espana, Manila from 8 AM to noon, sometimes extending until 2 PM. I'd listen intently to Mr. Martin's and Mr. Tan's lectures and take detailed notes in my NPTE logbook. After that, I'd conduct home health visits from 2 PM to 6 PM. I'd catch a quick nap from 7 PM to 9:30 PM before starting the cycle all over again. After that, I'd do home health visits from 2 PM to 6 PM. I'd catch a quick nap from 7 PM to 9:30 PM before starting the cycle again. My mom still packed my meals—rice and scrambled eggs tucked into reused shopping bags. During my 3 AM break at the call center, I'd heat up the food and pair it with coffee (thanks to the free microwave and coffee maker provided). Each bite reminded me why I was pushing so hard.

The review center was filled with dreamers like me, all convinced America would solve our problems. We'd share handwritten notes on logbooks to save money, quiz each other on the jeepney, and dream about dollar salaries. "*When I get to America,*" sometimes becomes a prefix to a sentence. "*When I get to America, I'll buy a car. When I get to America, I'll send money home. When I get to America, everything will be different.*"

I passed the TOEFL on my first try—those call center nights had prepared me well. The FCCPT credentials took six months of back-and-forth documentation. Then came the biggest hurdle: getting a tourist visa to take the NPTE in America. The embassy interview was terrifying. They assumed everyone wanted to illegally stay. I had to prove I had reasons to return to the Philippines—a job (which I was planning to leave), and family ties (which wouldn't stop me from staying if I wanted to).

Miraculously, they approved my visa application. In April 2013, I flew to Los Angeles—one of the few times I had boarded an airplane and left the Philippines, and it was my first time experiencing weather below 60°F. LAX (Los Angeles International

Airport) was overwhelming: clean, organized, and expensive. A bottle of water cost $3—more than my daily allowance back home. I stayed in a Best Western hotel in Inglewood, California, all paid for by my sponsoring agency, sharing a room with another one of my colleagues. Breakfast was included, so I would set aside some leftover sausage patties during our short stay while we were preparing for the NPTE.

The testing center was a few miles away from the hotel and the agency who sponsored our flight told us to just book a taxi as a group to make sure we all got there in time. Two hundred and fifty exam questions that would determine my future. I finished in three hours, my hands shaking as I clicked 'submit'. The results would come in 14 days.

Right after my exam, my roommate's uncle and his family kindly welcomed us to stay at their home for a week, and treated us to a free tour of iconic Los Angeles spots—Hollywood Boulevard, the Walk of Fame, and Griffith Observatory. His aunt even brought us along to their annual Kaiser celebration at Universal Studios, which was so much fun! Everything in LA felt huge and spread out; you really needed a car to get around. The city was a mix of contrasts—homeless people lived near million-dollar homes, and immigrants owned businesses with their names proudly displayed on the buildings. It was a chaotic yet exciting place, full of opportunities. I returned home to wait for my results.

One day at almost noon, Philippine time, I got a text from my agency: I passed! I was living at my grandparents' house, and my parents and I jumped around like we'd won the lottery. My siblings were at school when the news came.

CHAPTER 7

My Texas Beginning

Ten months later, around midnight in early March 2014 during a rainy night, I had a phone interview with a kind man from Fort Worth. He offered me a job as a therapist in East Texas, impressed by my work experience and potential. I happily accepted. By the last week of March, I arrived at Dallas/Fort Worth International Airport with just one suitcase, a balikbayan box, and a work contract from Health Carousel Passport USA. The company placed me in a skilled nursing facility in a small East Texas town with a population of 12,000.

The culture shock hit me right away. Everything was so spread out—the nearest grocery store was three miles away, and there was no public transport. My coworkers were friendly but unfamiliar with my background, asking things like, *"Where's the Philippines located?" "Do you have internet there?"* or saying, *"Your English is really good!"* The Mexican maintenance worker at the facility nicknamed me *"Manny"* after Manny Pacquiao, the famous Filipino boxer.

The agency gave me a reimbursement and signing bonus totaling nearly $2,000—more money than I'd ever had at one time. I saved most of it for a down payment on an apartment. I bought a basic bicycle from Walmart for $89. A month after starting work at the nursing facility, I called Wells Fargo—where my agency and I had already opened checking and savings accounts the day after I arrived at Dallas/Fort Worth Airport—to set up a brokerage account.

But I knew the clock was ticking. My H-1B visa was tied to my employer. If I lost my job or the company folded (which Sava eventually did post-pandemic), I'd have to leave the country. I needed to build wealth fast.

I practiced extreme frugality to save money. While my American coworkers spent $5 on coffee and $12 on lunches, I lived as if I was still in Manila. I brought homemade meals cooked with a rice cooker to work and biked seven miles to the job through the scorching 105°F Texas summer heat. My apartment had no air conditioning for cooling or heating, and I rotated the same five sets of scrubs. My only indulgence was a $60 monthly internet bill, essential for starting my transitional Doctor of Physical Therapy course. I also bought a desktop computer and a good Altec Lansing speaker for my daily YouTube watching.

My first Wells Fargo investment was $100 in Apple stock. The commission was $8—an 8% fee just to buy. Selling would cost another $8. I'd need the stock to rise 16% just to break even. It was excessive, but it was access. Every month, I'd add another $100, then $200, then $500. The commissions ate thousands annually—$2,000 to $3,000—but I was building something.

In 2016, Robinhood launched with zero commissions. I applied immediately. I was rejected: they only accepted permanent residents or citizens. My H-1B visa made me ineligible. Another door closed because of my immigration status.

But I kept going despite the challenges. During the day, I worked with elderly patients recovering from strokes and surgeries. At night, I studied the stock market—reading financial reports, watching Bloomberg, and learning about its history and fluctuations. I also enrolled in a Doctor of Physical Therapy program, partly to gain knowledge but mostly because the degree would help me secure a green card for permanent residency years later.

CHAPTER 8

My Grandfather's Last Lesson

In 2016, my grandfather passed away. His funeral was my first trip back to the Philippines since moving away. Seeing him in a suit before the cremation hit me hard, reminding me that life has its limits.

At the wake, relatives shared stories about him. My grandfather was a quiet man, not one for many words. I remembered him staying up late, waiting for me to get home from school or from playing basketball or Defense of the Ancients at a computer shop with my college friends. If I was out past 10 PM, he'd call my cellphone, calmly asking where I was. When I got home late, I'd find him watching Chinese news on TV, sitting in his white monoblock chair. My sweet grandmother would scold me, saying he hadn't eaten dinner or slept because he was waiting for me, urging me to be more considerate.

His accomplishments were impressive, especially for someone not born in the Philippines. He'd bought the house we lived in outright and purchased lots for my father's siblings to build their own homes. He also had a savings account that earned annual interest. I recalled him checking interest rates in Chinese newspapers weekly, quietly grumbling that they'd dropped from a high of 20% years ago to almost nothing now.

After the funeral, I returned to Texas with a new perspective. Real estate—that was the key I'd been missing.

PART THREE:
My Real Estate Revelation

CHAPTER 9

My Cleveland Discovery

By early 2020, my stock portfolio had grown to nearly $200,000—a fortune by Philippine standards, but modest by American ones. I could feel the market getting frothy. Tesla was trading at insane multiples. People were day-trading on their phones.

Then came March 2020: COVID-19, lockdowns, and the market crash. My portfolio dropped to less than $100,000 in just three weeks. I didn't sell—Buffett's training held—but watching those numbers evaporate daily was agony. Worse, my facility became a death trap. Patients were dying weekly. Coworkers were calling in sick and never returning. I was working my usual schedule, donning a hazmat suit and well-worn and recycled n95 respirator, being notified of numerous patients having passed away, and wondering if I'd be next.

The government's response was to print money. Stimulus checks, the Paycheck Protection Program (PPP) loans, and most importantly, the Federal Reserve cut interest rates to zero. Mortgage rates plummeted below 3%—the lowest in American history. This resulted in the fastest stock market recovery, and almost instantly my portfolio was back to its previous gains and then some. I did not believe that the market could keep rising despite the fact that no vaccine was being developed that summer, so I was eager to sell my gains and diversify.

In June 2020, stuck in my apartment during another lockdown weekend, I read a *Wall Street Journal* article that changed my life: "*Cleveland Is a House-Flipping Hot Spot, and Covid Adds Fuel.*"[3] It profiled a single mother buying distressed properties in Cleveland for $40,000, renovating them, and selling them for $160,000. But one detail stood out: she also sold to out-of-state investors who kept them as rentals.

Cleveland? I'd never been there. But the numbers were staggering. Houses for under $200,000 that rented for $1,500 monthly. The rent-to-price ratio was 0.75%—in expensive cities, it was 0.3%. You could actually generate cash flow from day one.

I did a Google search and ended up at the Real Wealth Network website, which provided me with the contact details of the fixer-upper lady featured in the Journal article. I emailed the woman profiled in the article that same day through the real estate website. "*I'm an investor from Texas interested in Cleveland properties.*" (Investor was a stretch—I was a physical therapist with a brokerage

---

[3] https://www.wsj.com/articles/cleveland-is-a-house-flipping-hot-spot-and-covid-is-helping- 11591629995

account.) One of her sales agents replied within hours. She had a duplex available. Just renovated. $160,000. Both units rented at $850 each.

I opened my calculator:

- Purchase price: $160,000.
- Down payment (25%): $40,000.
- Monthly rent: $1,700.
- Estimated monthly mortgage payment: $950.
- Cash flow: $750 monthly.

The return on my $40,000 would be 22.5% annually. The stock market averaged 10%.

CHAPTER 10

The First Deal

Buying a property 1,200 miles away was daunting—I'd never seen the place, visited the city, or met the seller. During those isolating times, I kept my plans quiet. If I'd told anyone, they'd probably have said, *"Cleveland? Why not just burn your money?"*

But my grandfather taught me a key lesson: while others hesitate, the brave take action. I remembered how he invested nearly $1,000 (in today's money) to help me join a physical therapy clinic less than a year after I graduated. That clinic was a partnership between my college friends, former clinical supervisors, and professors, with no proven business success. Even in 2014, as I prepared to leave for the land of milk and honey, he was still checking on that investment.

The biggest challenge for my first real estate deal was getting finance. Banks required two years of tax returns to prove steady income, a credit score above 740, and detailed explanations for every deposit, withdrawal, and financial decision. Most crucially, they wanted proof that my credit card balances were paid off and clarity on where the money to pay them came from. And most importantly, they wanted to know my immigration status.

To make it clear, I had just obtained my green card in early 2020 just before the lockdown.

Happily, most of the banks recommended by the seller of the investment property were experienced in financing these types of properties. They focused more on my ability to repay the loan rather than my status as a green card holder or citizen.

Finally, a mortgage broker in Ohio who worked with out-of-state investors agreed to help. The rate would be 3.2%—higher than the advertised 2.7%, but still historically low. The catch: I needed 25% down plus closing costs—about $50,000 in total.

Selling stocks in August 2020 felt like betrayal. The market was recovering. Tesla was soaring. But I remembered Kiyosaki: *"Rich people acquire assets. The poor and middle class acquire liabilities that they think are assets."* Stocks were paper. Real estate was real.

The inspection report was a clear, one-page document listing eight issues, with the seller noting they would fix each before closing. These included a sloping foundation, an old roof, electrical problems, and plumbing concerns. However, the seller had already addressed other major issues. The property was an 1875 Victorian duplex, so it would always have some problems—that's why it generated good cash flow.

On August 14, 2020, I wired $45,984.09 to a title company in Cleveland for a building I'd only seen in pictures. The money came from selling part of my stock portfolio, which had earned strong returns, to diversify my investments. If this turned out to be a scam, I'd have to start from scratch at age 32.

On August 17, 2020, the title company sent a notary to my apartment to sign the documents finalizing the purchase. After signing, the notary said, *"Congratulations, you're now a landlord!"* The keys to the duplex were given to the property manager recommended by the seller. The duplex at Sackett Avenue, Cleveland, Ohio, had two units, four bedrooms, and two bathrooms. Built when Ulysses S. Grant was president, it is now mine.

CHAPTER 11

The McAllen Mistake

The duplex closing gave me confidence. Too much confidence. I immediately started hunting for my next deal, this time closer to my home state. McAllen, Texas, on the Mexican border, had the right numbers. Plus, with a Federal Housing Administration (FHA) loan, I could buy a primary residence with just 3.5% down.

This is the hack nobody tells immigrants: FHA loans are available to anyone with legal work authorization. You don't need a green card. You don't need perfect credit. You only need a valid visa and a pulse. With $500,000 in buying power and just $17,500 down, you could buy a mansion. Or in my case, you could buy a disaster.

The listing looked perfect: three bedrooms, two baths, corner lot, $87,500. *"Handyman special!"* the ad said cheerfully. *"Great bones!"* What it should have said was, *"Money pit with foundation issues!"*

Like the duplex purchase, I didn't physically visit the McAllen house. During the lockdowns, I hired an inspector recommended by the seller's realtor to conduct a detailed inspection and list any issues. The seller's agent, found through Redfin, was enthusiastic. The inspector, also recommended by the agent, was seemingly very thorough, noting 13 items. One item, number 22, casually mentioned, *"Observed floor appeared to slope to right side. Saw no signs of current structural movement at time of inspection."* No mention was made of the foundation or any foundational issues.

I offered $69,000; they countered at $90,000. We settled on $87,500. With the FHA loan, my down payment was only $3,062, and closing costs brought my total investment to about $4,375. We closed the week after I had closed on the duplex. I told the bank it would be my primary residence, and was planning to move in right after closing. (And I did—eventually—packing up my apartment with help from my buddies in Mt. Pleasant and Brownsboro, Texas, and driving 12 hours with bathroom breaks for me and my two German Shepherds from East Texas to South Texas.)

In the first month, I learned why the floors sloped: the pier and beam foundation was shot. Not settling—crumbling. The living room tilted so much I could slide from the bedroom to the kitchen without walking. Repair estimates? At least $15,000. I knew nothing about foundations until I Googled an expert for a quote.

Here's a lesson worth $15,000: NEVER buy a house with a pier and beam foundation.

They're obsolete technology, impossible to finance repairs for, and a nightmare to maintain. But I was already committed. In short, avoid this type of foundation at all costs.

The foundation repair took a month—not because of the work itself, but because the experts were booked solid. Their offer came with a lifetime guarantee, which sold me despite the wait. I bought this fixer-upper knowing it could be modernized. I hired a Mexican contractor, recommended by a local Filipino realtor, who had all his tools in his van. For $1,000 a week, he tackled interior and exterior teardown, plus painting, electrical, and plumbing fixes while I stayed working seven days a week. But then he had found more issues: 1960s plumbing, sketchy electrical work, and an HVAC (heating, ventilation and air conditioning) system that died on day 90. By the time the house was livable, I'd sunk another $55,000 into a property worth about $90,000:

- Total investment: $59,375.
- Monthly mortgage payment: $1,200.
- Eventual monthly rent: $1,100.
- Monthly loss: $100.

My first negative cash flow property. But it taught me invaluable lessons: inspect everything twice, budget for repairs then double it, and location matters less than condition.

PART FOUR: Scaling the Portfolio

CHAPTER 12

The Eight-Door Gamble

By late 2020, I was fully consumed by real estate fever. The Cleveland duplex was stabilizing, though barely—one unit was often vacant. The McAllen house was bleeding money but teaching me about renovations while serving as my home. I wanted more. Bigger properties. That way, when the mortgage is paid off, the rent would roll in by the multiples. I had my sights set on apartment complexes.

Brandon Turner from the Bigger Pockets podcast had bought out his landlord's apartment building. I tried the same with my East Texas complex—I cold-called the elderly couple who owned it, and offered to buy them out. They politely declined.

Commercial loans are different beasts. Residential mortgages (one to four units) are standardized, government-backed, 30-year fixed instruments. Commercial loans (five+ units) are portfolio products—banks keep them in-house, terms are negotiable, and they require 25–30% down. Most importantly, they required an LLC (limited liability company). I was buying as a business now, not as a person.

I formed my own LLC in December 2020 to meet lender demands and to qualify for a commercial loan.

Through my Cleveland realtor (we were acquaintances by now, despite not meeting in person and communicating mainly via email—she had made a decent commission from my first duplex and referred me to a commercial lending broker), I initially looked close to my neighborhood, or at least near McAllen, Texas. I found a decent mom-and-pop-run apartment complex nearly three hours north—an eight-unit apartment selling for $560,000 that reportedly collected $5,700 monthly from all units. I obtained pre-approval from the referred mortgage broker. The broker later proposed a deal that had fallen through in Cleveland.

That's when I found it: an eight-unit apartment complex in Cleveland for $400,000. The current rent roll was $5,090 monthly. With room to raise rents, I could get to $5,960. The math was beautiful:

- Down payment: $100,000.
- Monthly mortgage (6.625% commercial rate): $1,940.
- Monthly rent: $5,090.
- Cash flow: $3,000+ monthly.

The problem: I needed $100,000 cash plus closing costs. My stock portfolio was recovering after the initial withdrawal for the duplex and now worth close to $200,000 again. But selling in November 2020 felt insane—we'd just had the vaccine announcement, and markets were soaring. But I remembered my grandfather: *"Money is like a river. It must keep flowing."*

I sold $120,000 in stocks. Apple, Microsoft, and several regional banks that were publicly listed—all at what seemed like peaks (they'd double within a year, but you can't think like that). The wire to the title company was the largest transaction of my life: $115,000 for an eight-unit building in a city I'd never visited.

February 2021: I became the owner of 7712 Lawn Avenue, Cleveland, Ohio. Eight units. Sixteen bedrooms. Eight bathrooms. A proper apartment building. I was a real estate mogul (in my head).

CHAPTER 13

The Property Manager Education

Reality hit immediately. Three tenants were behind on rent. One unit had been vacant for six months. The previous owner had been managing it himself, keeping paper records in a shoebox. Section 8 inspections (for government-subsidized, low-income tenants) were failing. The city was sending violation notices.

I hired a property management company—charging 12% of gross rents, plus placement fees, plus maintenance markups. They were professional slackers, but necessary ones. From Texas, I couldn't handle midnight toilet emergencies or serve eviction notices.

The first year was educational:

- Tenant screening is everything. Previous convictions, previous evictions, previous late payments are all predictive.

- Section 8 is a blessing and curse. It provides guaranteed government rent payments, but tenants who know they're judgment-proof.
- Maintenance is constant. Eight units means something breaks weekly.
- Vacancy is death. One empty unit in eight is a 12.5% revenue loss.

Here are the numbers:

- 2021 revenue: $46,800.
- 2021 expenses: $28,000.
- 2021 cash flow: $18,800 ($1,566 per month).
- Cash-on-cash return: 18.8%.

Not the 22% I'd projected, but better than stocks that year. I was learning that real estate projections are fantasy—reality is always 20% worse.

One thing I found out about property management is that you must hire slowly and fire fast. Nonetheless, I believe I found the best landlord and caretakers of my property despite the tough times that ensued from owning these out-of-state properties. Shout out to you, Bridget and Erik.

CHAPTER 14

The Tax Disaster

In 2023, I received a letter that nearly ended my real estate career: a Cuyahoga County tax reassessment. My eight-unit property, previously assessed at $120,000, was now valued at $400,000—its purchase price. My taxes were jumping from $6,865 annually to $13,982. Plus, I owed back taxes for 2021 and 2022.

Nearly $14,000 a year. That's $1,165 monthly—almost my entire mortgage payment, just for taxes.

I called the county assessor's office, furious. How was this legal? How could taxes spike so suddenly? The clerk was unmoved. "You bought it for $400,000. That's the market value. Pay up or face penalties."

My mortgage servicer had been collecting escrow based on the old assessment, paying the lower amount, assuming it was correct. Now they demanded $17,663 immediately to cover the shortfall, plus an increased monthly payment for future taxes. The previous property manager had also let tenants sign my LLC's name on their utility bills. I was out $25,000 immediately.

My monthly escrow payment soared from $3,246 to $6,473. My monthly cash flow flipped from a $1,566 surplus to a $2,500 deficit. I was bleeding money.

My fiancée and I welcomed our first child in January 2024. After a period of pure happiness and bliss as we welcomed parenthood, February 2024 became my lowest point. I was working seven days a week to cover the shortfall. We'd just bought a house in Dallas with a $3,600 mortgage, and now our Cleveland property demanded another $3,227 monthly. Where would I find $6,827 a month just for mortgages?

I nearly broke down. I called the servicer threatening bankruptcy. After frantic negotiations with both the county and my mortgage servicer, I sent my last $10,000 in savings to reduce the monthly payment to $4,744. Those crushing payments forced me to maintain my seven- day work week in both nursing facilities and hospitals, even with our newborn daughter at home.

By 2025, escrow dropped to $3,705 per month. The apartment was still losing about $22,000 annually (about $1,833 per month), but at least I wasn't hemorrhaging my entire salary.

The irony? Despite the disaster, the apartment's rent roll was climbing—from $46,800 in 2021 to $57,695.99 in 2024—a 23% increase. If I could survive the tax hit and secure a decent 30-year, fixed-rate refinance by early 2026, the property might actually work long- term.

Some days, staring at my spreadsheets, I wondered if I should've stuck with stocks. The S&P 500 averaged 12.26% annual returns during this period. My $100,000 down payment would've grown to $140,000 by 2024, with zero headaches about mortgage payments.

CHAPTER 15

The Dallas Delusion

Despite the Cleveland tax nightmare, we bought a house in Dallas in September 2023. This wasn't an investment—it was for our growing family. But, of course, I couldn't help thinking like an investor.

The logic seemed solid:

- New build in a gated community (Dallas has serious crime issues).
- Pulte construction (better than Lennar or D.R. Horton).
- 10–15 minutes from downtown.
- Builder financing at 5.8% when market rates were over 7%.
- Primary bedroom downstairs (key for future rental potential).
- Purchase price: $450,000. Down payment (10%): $45,000 (my fiancée contributed half). Monthly mortgage: $3,600 (split equally with my fiancée).

But I got greedy. I spent my own $30,000 on *"luxury"* upgrades: gold fixtures, designer mirrors, premium ceiling fans, and smart-home everything. I convinced myself these upgrades would fetch premium rent when we moved out.

The house was stunning—soaring ceilings, a corner lot, and walking distance to White Rock Lake. It looked like a magazine spread. We lived there for exactly one year.

Dallas's problems emerged slowly. Car break-ins were routine. The Planet Fitness gym on Buckner Boulevard in Mesquite, Texas, had a parking lot plagued by a theft ring. Homeless camps appeared under highway overpasses. The diversity we'd sought felt more like division—racial tension was palpable. This wasn't where we wanted to raise our daughter, Aria.

When I listed it for rent, reality hit hard. My dream rent: $4,800 monthly (including utilities). After six weeks of silence, except for spam callers, I got $2,900 monthly (no utilities). The luxury upgrades meant nothing. Location and square footage were all that mattered:

- Monthly mortgage: $3,400.
- Monthly rent: $2,900.
- Monthly loss: $700.
- Cash-on-cash return: negative 13.33%.

My worst deal yet. The $40,000 in upgrades might as well have been burned.

Lesson learned: never upgrade a rental beyond basic functionality. Tenants don't pay for champagne taste.

PART FIVE: Lessons from the Trenches

CHAPTER 16

The Numbers That Matter (And the Ones That Don't)

Let me show you the real numbers—not the glossy projections real estate gurus sell, but the actual profit and loss statements that determine whether you eat or declare bankruptcy.

Cleveland Duplex (Purchased September 2020 for $160,000)

2023 Reality:

- Rent collected: $4,080 (supposed to be $20,400).
- Expenses: $6,785.
- Mortgage payments: $12,100.
- Total loss: $14,805.

2024 Improvement:

- Rent collected: $21,000.
- Expenses: $10,844.
- Mortgage payments: $12,564.
- Total loss: $2,410.

It took 41 months—3.4 years—before this property stabilized. Three-and-a-half years of bleeding money, fielding midnight calls, dealing with evictions, and questioning my sanity. The real estate books don't mention that timeline.

McAllen House (Purchased September 2020 for $87,500)

- Total investment after repairs: $60,500.
- Monthly mortgage: $1,200.
- Monthly rent: $1,100.
- Monthly loss: $100.
- Annual loss: $1,200.

A negative 2% return. I would have been better off buying Treasury bonds.

Cleveland Apartment (Purchased February 2021 for $400,000)

2024—The Disaster Year:

- Rent collected: $55,995.
- Operating expenses: $33,720.

- Mortgage payments: $56,938.
- Special tax payment to servicer: $10,000,
- Total loss: $44,663.

$44,000 lost in one year. That's a median American salary, gone. But here's what the numbers don't show:

- The tenant who paid three months late but included a Christmas card thanking me for not evicting her during cancer treatment.
- The pride when a tenant's kid graduated high school and said my affordable rent helped them save for college.

I'm kidding—none of that happened. AI made it up.

CHAPTER 17

What They Don't Tell You About Being a Landlord

Real estate influencers sell passive income dreams. *"Mailbox money,"* they call it. *"Make money while you sleep."* Here's what actually happens while you sleep.

The Thanksgiving Education

November 29, 2023, 9:22 AM, Wednesday: *"The entire front porch of the Sackett property collapsed."* Someone crashed into it last night, then fled. *"We're filing a police report,"* my property manager told me as I was trying to figure out where to get our turkey for the next day's big meal.

Cost: $5,878. Insurance coverage: $0 (I didn't want my premium to rise significantly).

"Life is not easy, it is not. Don't try to make it that way. Life is not fair, it never was, it isn't now, and it won't ever be." Matthew McConaughey

The Section 8 Paradox

Section 8 is government-subsidized housing—the government pays part or all of the tenant's rent directly to you. Sounds perfect, right? Guaranteed payment from Uncle Sam. Here's the reality.

Pros:
- Payment arrives on the first of every month via automatic deposit.
- No chasing tenants for rent.
- No bounced checks.

Cons:
- Annual inspections that can fail for simple reasons (for example, light and faucet replacements, caulking of shower tiles).
- Tenants who know they're judgment-proof—you can't garnish (i.e., legally seize) government benefits.
- If they damage your property, good luck collecting.
- The stigma that keeps good tenants away.

One of my Section 8 tenants in Cleveland disappeared in August 2024. I later found out he'd been arrested. Left behind: a unit that looked like a crime scene (it might have been), $6,000 in damages, and three months of cleanup.

The Property Management Tax

Property managers charge 8–12% of gross rents. For my Cleveland apartment, that's $400–$600 monthly. Here's what you actually get:

- Someone to ignore tenant calls until they contact you directly.
- Maintenance charges and management fees to ensure repairs are delivered.
- Placement fees of one month's rent for finding tenants.
- The privilege of still handling some major repair decisions yourself.

But here's the thing: from 1,200 miles away, hiring a property manager is the only way to keep my sanity while 'landlording' 10 tenants and their families. I can't serve eviction notices from Texas. I can't show units on weekends. I can't fix toilets at midnight. So, I pay the price and pretend it's not overspending.

CHAPTER 18

The Psychology of Losing Money

Nobody talks about what losing $44,663 in a year does to your psyche. These aren't paper losses in the stock market that might recover. This is real money draining from your bank account monthly, relentlessly, while you work seven days a week to cover the gap.

In February 2024, after the tax bomb, I considered selling my Cleveland apartment at a loss—just keep making payments until someone saw my lackluster numbers as an attractive investment. The apartment was worth about $400,000. I owed $300,000. After selling costs, I might clear $70,000—less than my down payment. Four years of stress for a $30,000 loss.

But walking away meant admitting failure. It meant my grandfather's ghost would haunt me. It meant all those books about persistence were wrong. It meant I was just another overleveraged speculator crushed by reality.

So, I developed coping mechanisms:

- **The 10-Year View**: In a decade, the mortgage will be partially paid down, rents will likely rise, and the tax situation might stabilize. Maybe I'll break even by 2034. (This is delusional optimism, but it helps.)
- **The Forced Savings Account**: Each month, tenants pay down my loan principal—about $500 monthly across all properties, or $6,000 annually in equity I wouldn't otherwise have.
- **The Diversification appeal**: I tell myself that real estate diversifies my investment portfolio beyond stocks—a different asset class, with a different risk profile. Stocks are paper assets; real estate properties are tangible assets.
- **The Learning Experience**: Every disaster teaches something. Foundation issues taught me about inspections. Tax reassessments taught me due diligence. Vacancies taught me tenant screening. (At $44,663 a year, this is the world's priciest education.)

CHAPTER 19

Why I Haven't Quit (Yet)

Given the numbers, any rational person would ask: Why continue? Why not sell everything, put it back in index funds, and sleep peacefully? Here's why.

The Immigration Math

As an immigrant, I think differently about generational wealth. My grandfather built a business that supported three generations. In America, real estate is the equivalent—a tangible asset that survives immigration, currency changes, and political upheaval.

My daughter Aria is an American citizen by birth. These properties, despite their current losses, are her inheritance. In 30 years, when the mortgages are paid off, she'll own:

- A duplex in Cleveland.

- A house in McAllen.
- An eight-unit apartment in Cleveland.
- A house in Dallas.
- A new build in Dallas suburb.

They will be free and clear real estate generating maybe $15,000 monthly. That's $180,000 annually in passive income. That's freedom.

The Refinancing Hope

My Cleveland apartment's commercial loan expires in 2026. If I can refinance to a 30-year fixed rate at even 8 or 9%, then my payment would also be fixed. With annual rent increases, the property will become cash-flow positive. The nightmare will end.

The Rent Growth Reality

Despite everything, rents keep rising:

- Cleveland duplex: $850/unit (2020) to $875/unit (2024).
- Cleveland apartment: $550/unit (2021) to $700/unit (2024).
- McAllen house: $1,300 (2021) to $1,100 (2025)—okay, that one went down (mainly because I am no longer paying for electricity, internet, and water utilities).
- Dallas house: $0 (lived in it) to $2,900 (2024).
- Dallas suburb house: $0 (will be living in it).

Inflation is the landlord's friend. As the dollar weakens, rents rise, but mortgages stay fixed. In 10 years, today's disaster might be tomorrow's goldmine.

The Property Value Rollercoaster

- Cleveland duplex: $160,000 (2020) to $205,000 (2025), a 28.13% increase.
- Cleveland apartment: $400,000 (2021) to $670,000 (2025), a 67.50% increase. Apartments are being valued by the designated capitalization rate and the rent per door. Basically, the higher the rent, the higher the apartment value becomes.
- McAllen house: $87,500 (2020) to $164,000 (2025), an 87.43% increase.
- Dallas house: $450,000 (2023) to $447,000 (2025), a 0.67% decrease.

"If it makes sense, it makes dollars, BABY!"
Ben Mallah

The Ego Factor

Let's be honest: I can't admit defeat. I told myself my *annus horribilis*—2024—had passed, and I'd survived into 2025. This won't be the end of me in this brutal real estate business. I'll hold on tight for at least five more years and decide by 2030 whether to sell these assets.

My struggles even caught media attention. The *Wall Street Journal* featured professionals like me in *"The Upper Middle Class Is Getting*

Squeezed"—physical therapists, supposedly successful, drowning in property payments and childcare costs while working seven days a week.[4]

PERSONAL FINANCE

The Upper Middle Class Is Getting Squeezed

The first two years of the pandemic were good for the group's savings and investments, but 2022 isn't

By Dion Rabouin [Follow] | Photographs by Dina Litovsky for The Wall Street Journal
July 25, 2022 5:30 am ET

Mark Yu had a profitable pandemic. Like many Americans, he added to his savings and pulled in big gains from the stock-market rally. He purchased a house in his new hometown of McAllen, Texas, then a duplex and an eight-unit apartment complex in Cleveland.

But 2022 hasn't been so kind. His expenses have grown because of higher costs for gas, groceries and the dog food for his four German shepherds. The value of his stockholdings is shrinking. He is sending more money back to his family in the Philippines to help them cope with rising prices there. A cracked foundation in his new house cost tens of thousands of dollars to repair.

Mr. Yu, a 33-year-old who has lived in the U.S. since 2014, is now taking on credit-card debt and typically working seven days a week. Previously, he was socking away as much as $3,000 a month into a brokerage account. This year, a couple-hundred is the most he had been able to muster and he hasn't put anything in for the past three months.

His story is similar to that of a number of upper-middle-class Americans who are seeing their two years of pandemic gains eroded.

> "We were playing the game 'pretend and extend.' Now that period is over, they have moved to 'pray and delay.' What happens after you pray and delay? The s---'s going to hit the fan." Ben Mallah On The 2024 Housing Bubble, Getting Rich, & Going Broke[6]

---

4   https://www.wsj.com/personal-finance/the-upper-middle-class-is-getting-squeezed-11658741402

CHAPTER 20

What I'd Do Differently

If I could go back to 2020 with today's knowledge, here's what I'd change.

1. Never Buy Without Visiting

The Cleveland duplex, bought sight unseen, has been a nightmare. The McAllen house, which I did not tour, has been manageable. Seeing a property reveals things that photos hide, like the neighborhood feel, and the critical $15,000 foundation issues.

2. Budget 2X for Repairs

It's not just that contractors or handymen who charge high rates; it's the cost of repairs combined with vacancies periods where you won't be earning rental income. And those periods can skyrocket when you hire an incompetent handyman.

3. Avoid Pier and Beam Foundations

It's worth repeating: NEVER buy pier and beam. They're 1950s technology that no modern lender wants to finance repairs for. If you have one pier and beam foundation issue, then you will be paying cash for fixes that cost more than the house.

4. Ignore Cash-on-Cash (CoC) Returns

Every real estate calculator shows amazing CoC returns by ignoring reality:

- Vacancy periods (assume 20% minimum).
- Repairs (assume 20% of rent).
- Property management (10 to 15% of rent).
- Capital expenditures (new roof, HVAC—budget 10% of rent).
- Tax increases (assume 5% annually).

Real returns are half of projections. If the numbers don't work at 50% of the projected return, then don't buy.

5. Location Matters More Than Price

My Cleveland properties were cheap but they are in C-class neighborhoods. Higher crime, higher turnover, more evictions, and more repairs. The Dallas house is in a B-class area but is too expensive to generate cash flow. Despite this, I still believe that the sweet spot is a property at an average price in B-class, working-class neighborhoods with stable tenants who pay rent and don't destroy property. But make sure to ask your realtor to get the comparable prices of other 3-bedroom or 2-bedroom homes in the area and not splurge like I did.

6. Never Upgrade Rentals

The $40,000 I spent on Dallas upgrades added maybe $100 to monthly rent. Tenants want functional, not fancy. Every dollar spent on aesthetics is wasted.

7. Commercial Loans Are Traps

My 5-year commercial loan seemed smart. But the adjustment risk is massive. When it resets in 2026, rates might be 10%. Always take a 30-year fixed rate whenever possible, even at higher rates. Certainty has value.

CHAPTER 21

The Immigrant Advantage

Despite the disasters, being an immigrant gave me advantages that American-born investors lack.

Comfort with Discomfort

Americans complain about 2-hour commutes. I did nine-hour shifts after a total of four-to- five-hour daily commutes in Manila traffic. Americans stress about $5,000 emergency funds. I survived on 60 pesos daily. The pain of negative cash flow doesn't compare to the pain of poverty.

Different Reference Points

My American colleagues think $2,000 monthly rent is expensive. In Manila, my family's house—which my grandfather owned outright—could rent for maybe $200 monthly. Every American rental, even my money-losers, generates wealth by Philippine standards. To think of this positively, I can plan ahead for retirement while generating rental income in dollars here and live lavishly in the future in the Philippines as a dual citizen. *"Suffer today, enjoy tomorrow,"* as Chinkee Tan says.

No Safety Net Means No Retreat

American-born investors can move back with their parents, declare bankruptcy, and start over. My H-1B visa meant that unemployment meant deportation. Failure meant returning to the Philippines with nothing. That fear drove me through the worst moments.

> *"Do not fall into the trap, the entitlement trap of feeling like you're a victim. You are not. Get over it and get on with it. And yes, most things are more rewarding when you break a sweat to get them back."* Matthew McConaughey

Currency Arbitrage Mindset

Every dollar earned in America is worth 50 pesos in the Philippines. My $44,000 loss in Cleveland is 2.2 million pesos—enough to buy a house in Manila with cash. This mental math makes losses bearable and gains spectacular. This is why I would not give up on my properties easily. That $15,000 monthly rental income is certainly a lofty goal, but not too far from achievable with all my current properties, given at least a 10-year vision.

Generational Thinking

Americans think in quarters and years. Immigrants think in generations. My grandfather built wealth over 60 years. I'm only 10 years into my American journey. The daily disasters matter less than the 50-year trajectory. Hindsight is 20/20. Everything will fall into alignment, eventually. Someday I will be that real estate mogul I believe I can become, for *"What our mind can conceive, our body can achieve,"* as Earl Nightingale said.

CHAPTER 22

The Philippines Detour

In October 2021, while the stock market hit new all-time highs, YouTube's algorithm fed me clips from a Filipino realtor's channel showcasing condominiums along EDSA in Metro Manila. The infomercial promised a simple condo unit for less than $200 a month in mortgage payments. *Why not diversify internationally?* I thought.

I contacted the realtor. As a Filipino citizen, the purchase seemed straightforward—until refinancing five years later. Being divorced in the U.S. but still legally married in the Philippines (civil marriages require a court order to recognize foreign divorces as annulments) turned into a bureaucratic nightmare. As I write this in August 2025, after flying to the Philippines in January, I'm still wrestling with red tape to refinance my remaining loan balance. The private company, part of the condominium monopoly in the Philippines, has been nearly unbearable to deal with.

Months later, peak stupidity hit. A college friend—honestly, a former crush—who'd become a condo sales agent sold me another property in Laguna. I was trying to impress her by buying another $200-a-month mortgage for a condominium in a far-flung area with *"potential"* for a future railway station from Manila. Both purchases happened in 2021, at the height of my real estate fever.

My goal is to eventually rent these units out for profit via short-term Airbnb, leveraging their amenities: swimming pool, kiddie pool, fitness gym, outdoor fitness area, and function rooms.

CHAPTER 23

The Dallas Gambit and its Aftermath

By early 2022, my fiancée was complaining about our living situation in the South Texas fixer-upper. Since she'd moved in October 2021, challenges had mounted. I'd hired a full- time handyman for six months at $1,000 weekly in cash to fully renovate the property. We even had to camp in our carport for a week because fresh paint fumes triggered my asthma. The population, culture, and lifestyle of McAllen just didn't match my fiancée's wants.

We started planning our move to Dallas. Houston floods too often, San Antonio felt too similar to McAllen, and Austin's prices were soaring as Californians invaded. Through NewHomeSource.com, I found a Pulte Homes build with soaring ceilings in a gated community. After our fixer-upper nightmare, we wanted nothing to do with secondhand homes.

Building commenced on our future home, and months later we discovered we were pregnant with Aria. Life-changing. I needed to step up my real estate game for my growing family. We drove 14 hours from McAllen to Coppell, Texas, to sign closing documents, stopping frequently for our four German Shepherds. The closing was anticlimactic—no coffee, no celebration, just signing our lives away for 30 years of payments. I had to ask the receptionist for the traditional photo with the oversized key.

Living in Dallas meant accepting lower healthcare pay—there were too many new graduates willing to work for less. Crime was rampant. Three weeks after moving in, someone smashed my Prius windows at Planet Fitness in Mesquite. Our friends who attended our housewarming mentioned checking school district rankings before buying—advice that came too late. Dallas had high crime and below-average school rankings in both math and English proficiency.

Then came the Cleveland catastrophe when Cuyahoga County hit me with those *"phantom taxes"*—back taxes from 2021 to 2023 with interest that I explained in Chapter 14.

CHAPTER 24

The California Experiment

In 2024, we made another dramatic move: California. The state that everyone is fleeing. The state with the highest taxes, the highest costs, and the highest everything, including the highest salaries.

I don't automatically ride trends—I test waters myself. Healthcare work made finding Bay Area jobs easy for both my fiancée and me.

My Texas physical therapy salary: $99,000.

My California physical therapy salary: $137,000—a 38% increase. The same work. The same hours. Substantially more money.

The plan was simple: work in California, and invest everywhere else. Geographic arbitrage. Earn in dollars, invest in distressed Midwest markets. The Cleveland apartment that nearly bankrupted me on a Texas salary suddenly became manageable on a California one.

And I've learned my lesson about buying property without understanding the market. The plan was to rent for two years, learn California's peculiarities, then maybe buy. Or maybe not. Sometimes the best investment is the one you don't make.

We're rented in California—$2,500 monthly for a one-bedroom apartment that would cost $1,100 in Texas. The salary differential more than covers it, but our other costs also skyrocketed proportionally. An example is daycare. In Dallas, daycare cost $350 weekly for our daughter. In California, it's $550 weekly—a 57% increase, or $2,200 monthly without holiday or weekend coverage. To put that monthly daycare payment into perspective, it's $600 more than my Cleveland duplex mortgage, and $1,000 more than my McAllen mortgage. I'm paying more for someone to watch my daughter than I pay for housing two families in Ohio.

So, four months into our California move, we started planning our return to Texas. It's not just the cost of living or the political atmosphere—it's the value proposition. In Texas, that same $2,500 monthly rent payment could buy us a 3,000-square-foot house in an A-rated school district. In California, it gets us 700 square feet and a view of a parking lot.

Don't misunderstand—California offers incredible benefits. The weather is perfect year-round. The mountains meet the ocean. My daughter's exposure to diversity and culture is invaluable. But when I run the numbers, when I think about building generational wealth, and when I consider where Aria will get the best education for our investment—Texas wins.

I started looking on NewHomeSource.com, eyeing a spacious new build in a Dallas suburb with A-rated schools and lake access as property number five. Because despite everything—the losses, the stress, the seven-day work weeks—I still believe real estate is the path.

Maybe I'm stubborn. Maybe I'm delusional. Or maybe I'm just an immigrant who knows that owning land in America, even land that loses money, is better than owning nothing at all.

CHAPTER 25

The Fifth Property— Dallas Suburb, Texas

In December 2024, while still living in California, we put an offer on our fifth property—a new build in a Dallas suburb, Texas. The purchase price: $750,000. This wasn't an investment property; this was our future home.

Why This House?

Three reasons drove this purchase:

First, the design captivated us. After years of living in fixer-uppers and cookie-cutter apartments, we wanted something beautiful. Something that felt like home the moment you walked in.

Second, the schools. The Dallas suburb house has an A-rated school district. Our Original Dallas house sits in a B-rated district, which would mean private school for Aria at $2,000–$2,500 monthly.

Instead of paying $30,000 annually for private education, we decided to buy in a better district. The higher mortgage essentially pays for itself through avoided tuition.

Third, timing. This would be our landing spot after our California experiment ends. A place to settle down, finally.

The Builder's Incentives

The housing market in 2024 was crawling. Builders were desperate. Our builder offered $15,000 cash toward closing costs through their preferred lender—similar to the $10,000 we'd received on our Dallas house. They promised 10–12 months for construction but finished in nine months, eager to close the sale.

I hired an inspector twice—once for the initial inspection, again a week later to verify repairs. With new builds, you get one chance to catch everything before you own it.

The Lending Nightmare

Here's where it nearly fell apart.

The lender initially told us we'd close August 22. I booked flights. I reserved a day at the Gaylord Resort in Irving to celebrate. Then they pushed the date. Then pushed it again. We finally closed September 5—two weeks late, after I'd already rescheduled everything twice.

The real problem was my debt-to-income ratio. Four properties with mortgages plus a new $750,000 house raised red flags. The lender demanded:

1. Three years of tax returns
2. Every bank statement
3. Every credit card statement
4. Rent rolls from all properties
5. Proof of rental income
6. An essay explaining my work history

They gave me two options:

1. Put down 25% ($190,000), or
2. Pay off my Cleveland duplex ($80,000 remaining) to reduce my debt load.

Neither option was acceptable.

After weeks of back-and-forth, with my fiancée as co-signer, we negotiated down to 10% ($75,000) by treating it as a second home rather than a primary residence. The irony—I had to prove I could afford a house I was buying specifically to save money on private school education.

The Closing

Despite the stress, watching Aria and my fiancée run through the empty rooms of our new 3,500-square-foot house made everything worth it. After five years of buying distressed properties, managing nightmare tenants, and losing money monthly, we finally had something beautiful. Something ours.

The numbers:

1. Purchase price: $750,000
2. Down payment: $75,000 (10%)
3. Builder incentive: $15,000
4. Monthly payment: approximately $5,200
5. Private school avoided: $2,500/month
6. Net additional cost: $2,700/month for a house we'll actually want to live in

For once, the math wasn't about cash flow or returns. It was about the quality of life. About giving Aria a stable home with good schools. About having a place where we're not landlords or investors—just a family.

Property number five might not make money, but it might make us happy. And after everything, maybe that's the better investment!

CHAPTER 26

The Trust and The Legacy

The end game isn't about me anymore. It's about Aria, and the children we might still have. I'm meeting with attorneys about creating a trust structure—a legal entity that will own all the properties and distribute income to my descendants.

The future trust and LLC structure will look like this:

- Mark Yu Living Trust (owns everything–eventually, I do not want to break any debt covenants until mortgages are paid off).
- Mark Yu Properties LLC (operates the McAllen, Cleveland, and Dallas houses).
- Mark Yu Philippine Holdings (operates both Philippine condos).

When I die, (hopefully a century from now ☺), the trust continues. No probate. No estate taxes (if structured correctly). No family fighting over properties. Just a machine that generates monthly income in perpetuity.

The attorney fees are $15,000. But it's infrastructure for generations.

I'm also exploring a real estate fund—raising money from other immigrants who want American real estate exposure but lack the knowledge or visa status to buy directly. The Cleveland disaster taught me the problems; maybe I can help others avoid them.

CHAPTER 27

The H-1B Reality Check

Let me share something about H-1B visas that nobody tells you upfront. Jason Calacanis said it best on his *"This Week in Startups"* podcast episode 2170: *"H-1B visa holders are going to get paid 30–40% less. They essentially become indentured servants. If they don't find a new job within 30 days of being laid off, they're kicked out of the country with their family."*

He continued: *"I have heard people explicitly in my career say, 'We're going to get these people because we can work them harder and they don't have any recourse.' To call them indentured servants may be hyperbolic, but they are significantly cheaper and less empowered workers."*[5]

---

5 https://podcasts.apple.com/ch/podcast/google-is-nano-banana-apple-ai-plans-the-great- h1b/id315114957?i=1000723805016

This was my reality from 2014 to 2020. My agency knew I couldn't leave. My employer knew I couldn't negotiate. When they relocated me from East Texas to Central Texas to another facility, I had no say. When they paid me less than American colleagues doing the same work, I smiled and accepted it.

There are several legal paths to American residency:

- H-1B work permit (temporary, employer-dependent).
- EB-2 green card (second preference, requires advanced degree).
- EB-3 green card (third preference, skilled workers).

Indians face decade-long backlogs. Filipinos wait five to seven years. Every day on an H-1B is a day wondering if you'll be sent home.

Here is my pathway to the green card/permanent residence in chronological order:

- **April 24, 2018**: I-140 (Immigrant Petition for Alien Worker) filed.
- **May 8, 2018**: Request for Evidence (RFE) issued for I-140.
- **July 12, 2018**: Request to withdraw I-140.
- **August 1, 2018**: I-140 case reopened.
- **August 2, 2018**: RFE response submitted for I-140.
- **August 3, 2018**: RFE response received by USCIS (United States Citizenship and Immigration Services).
- **August 15, 2018**: I-140 approved by USCIS.
- **August 24, 2018**: USCIS decision recorded for I-140.

- **October 11, 2018**: I-485 (Application to Adjust Status) filed.
- **November 1, 2018**: Notice of receipt for I-485 received.
- **November 30, 2018**: Biometrics appointment completed for I-485.
- **January 7, 2019**: Employment Authorization Document (EAD) received.
- **February 7, 2019**: Alternative reference to EAD receipt.
- **April 30, 2019**: I-485 adjustment of status interview conducted.
- **May 16, 2019**: EAD and Advance Parole approved.
- **May 20, 2019**: EAD card received.
- **May 27-31, 2019**: Alternative reference to I-485 interview.
- **July 11, 2019**: Interview notice received for I-485.
- **July 16, 2019**: I-485 interview scheduled in Irving, Texas.
- **August 9, 2019**: I-485 interview cancelled, and notice ordered.
- **December 20, 2019**: Mail received stating interview was cancelled, with new interview scheduled for January 10, 2020.
- **January 10, 2020**:
  - 8:00 AM: I-485 interview conducted.
  - 8:30 AM: I-485 interview completed.
- **January 11, 2020**: 11:00 AM: USCIS website updated stating 'New Card is Being Produced.'
- **January 14, 2020:** USCIS website updated 'Card Was Mailed to Me.'

- **January 14, 2020:** USCIS website updated 'Card Was Delivered to Me by the Post Office.'

EPILOGUE

Would I Do It Again?

It's 3 AM as I write this final chapter. Aria is crying in the next room—teething. My fiancée is exhausted from taking care of our family and working full-time. I'm exhausted from working weekends to cover negative cash flow. The Cleveland property manager just texted about lead paint and HVAC certification compliance for the apartment or running the risk of being penalised. The McAllen tenant is late on rent. The Dallas house has an HVAC issue.

By any objective measure, my real estate journey has been a failure. I've lost more money than I've made. I've aged 10 years in 5. I've stressed my relationship, postponed vacations, and missed family moments while dealing with property disasters.

But...

Every month, strangers pay down $500 to $2,000 of my mortgage principal. Every year, rents inch higher while mortgages stay fixed. Every decade, inflation erodes debt while enhancing asset values.

In 30 years, when Aria is my age, she'll inherit properties worth millions of dollars generating hundreds of thousands in annual income.

That's the intergenerational wealth my grandfather understood but never explicitly taught. That's the American dream reformulated for immigrants—not getting rich quick, but getting rich slowly, painfully, and inevitably.

Would I do it again? Ask me in 30 years. If Aria is financially free, if she never has to count pesos for jeepney fare or work graveyard shifts to pay for education, if she can pursue her passions without worrying about money—then yes, absolutely yes.

If not? Well, at least I'll have stories to tell and lessons to teach. And in the end, isn't that its own form of wealth?

FINAL THOUGHTS

As I finish this book, the sun is rising over California. My phone shows three new messages from property managers—probably more problems. My bank account shows another mortgage payment due. My spreadsheet shows another month of losses.

But my daughter is sleeping soundly in the next room with my loving fiancée. She has her toys neatly arranged in our tiny living room in our overpriced California apartment. She doesn't know that Daddy owns* five properties. She doesn't know about negative cash flow or tax reassessments or foundation repairs. She just knows she's loved, she's safe, and she's American.

That's the real return on investment. Everything else is just numbers on a spreadsheet.

To everyone who said it couldn't be done—you were almost right. To everyone who said it shouldn't be done—you were probably right. To everyone thinking about doing it anyway—welcome to the club.

The door is open. The opportunity is real. The pain is guaranteed. But so is the possibility.
Mark Yu California, 2025

APPENDIX A
The Real Numbers

For those who want the raw data, here's the actual performance of my first four properties over time:

Cleveland Duplex (Sackett Avenue)
- Purchase Price: $160,000
- Down Payment: $40,000
- Closing Costs: $8,000
- Total Investment: $48,000
- Monthly Mortgage: $950–$1,047
- Current Rent: $1,750 ($875/unit)
- 2024 Cash Flow: –$2,410
- Total Return Since 2020: –$34,000

McAllen House (Newport)
- Purchase Price: $87,500
- Down Payment: $5,000
- Repairs: $55,000

- Total Investment: $60,000
- Monthly Mortgage: $1,200
- Current Rent: $1,100
- Annual Cash Flow: -$1,200
- Total Return Since 2020: -$45,000

Cleveland Apartment (Lawn Avenue)

- Purchase Price: $400,000
- Down Payment: $100,000
- Closing Costs: $15,000
- Total Investment: $115,000
- Monthly Mortgage: $3,705 (2025)
- Current Rent: $4,666 ($583/unit)
- 2024 Cash Flow: -$44,663
- Total Return Since 2021: -$76,000

Dallas House (Sheboygan Avenue)

- Purchase Price: $450,000
- Down Payment: $45,000
- Upgrades: $40,000
- Total Investment: $85,000
- Monthly Mortgage: $3,900
- Current Rent: $2,900
- Annual Cash Flow: -$12,000
- Total Return Since 2023: -$24,000

Total Portfolio Performance

- Total Invested: $383,000
- Total Annual Cash Flow: –$59,863
- Total Return to Date: –$179,000
- Properties Owned: Five
- Units Owned: 12
- Total annual gross rent collection (2025 estimate): $124,992 ($10,416 a month)
- Current Portfolio Value: ~$1,847,500
- Current Portfolio Debt: ~$1,479,500
- Net Worth in Real Estate: ~$368,000

The numbers don't lie. I put in $383,000 and lost $179,000, for a net position of $368,000 after factoring in the current value of my first four properties and their combined current loan debt—almost exactly what I invested. Well, truthfully, it's a negative return over nearly five years. The S&P 500 would have turned that into $435,000 or more, given my aggressive approach to stock investing. This is not what you typically see from a successful real estate investment guru, nor am I claiming to be one. Nonetheless, I always keep track of my monthly gross rent and make sure that it grows over time to keep my mind sane and provide sound reasoning to just keep plowing ahead.

Real estate isn't for about five years. It's about 10, 20, 30, 40 years. And of course, I've just added a fifth property to my portfolio. Our dream home.

APPENDIX B

Lessons for Fellow Immigrants

If you're an immigrant considering U.S. real estate, here's what I wish someone had told me.

Visa Status Matters
- H1-B: You can buy property but have limited financing options.
- Green Card: You have full access to residential mortgages.
- Student Visa: You can buy but it's almost impossible to get finance.
- Tourist Visa: You can buy with cash only.

Credit Building Takes Time

- Open a secured credit card immediately upon your arrival.
- Never miss a payment—ever.
- Keep utilization below 30% of your credit limit.
- It takes two years to build sufficient credit for good mortgage rates.

FHA Loans Are Your Friend

- 3.5% down with a 580+ credit score.
- Available to any legal resident with work authorization.
- Can buy up to four units and live in one (i.e., house hack so that your tenant income pays for all or the majority of your unit's mortgage).
- The single best tool for immigrant investors.

Don't Trust the Gurus

- Their projected returns assume perfect conditions.
- They're selling courses, not teaching reality.
- Real returns are 50% less than projections.
- If it sounds too good to be true, it is.

Keep Your Day Job

- Real estate is not a passive investment.
- You need stable income for mortgage qualification.
- Properties will lose money initially.
- Plan for five years of losses before profits.

Think Generationally
- You might not get rich.
- Your children might.
- Your grandchildren definitely will.
- This is about legacy, not lifestyle.

ENDNOTES

1. TEDx Talks. (2016, April 14). *The skill of self-confidence | Dr. Ivan Joseph | TEDxRyersonU* [Video]. YouTube. https://www.youtube.com/watch?v=l03IX6op2Ec
2. Hill, N. (n.d.). *What the mind can conceive and believe, it can achieve.* Goodreads. https://www.goodreads.com/quotes/6641738-what-the-mind-can-conceive-and- believe-it-can-achieve
3. Grant, P. (2020, July 5). *Cleveland is a house-flipping hot spot, and Covid is helping.* The Wall Street Journal. https://www.wsj.com/articles/cleveland-is-a-house-flipping- hot-spot-and-covid-is-helping-1159162995
4. Lieber, R. (2022, July 15). *The upper middle class is getting squeezed.* The Wall Street Journal. https://www.wsj.com/personal-finance/the-upper-middle-class-is- getting-squeezed-11658741402
5. The Wall Street Journal. (2025, September 11). *Google is nano, banana, Apple AI plans, the great H1B* [Audio podcast episode]. In *WSJ Tech News Briefing*. Apple Podcasts. https://podcasts.apple.com/ch/podcast/google-is-nano-banana-apple-ai- plans-the-great-h1b/id315114957?i=1000723805016
6. The Iced Coffee Hour. (2024, October 14). *How to get rich in 2025 (step by step)* [Video]. YouTube. https://www.youtube.com/watch?v=YbmJjhBG56A&ab_channel=TheIcedCoffeeHour

ABOUT THE AUTHOR

The author is a Filipino-American real estate investor and entrepreneur whose journey from the streets of Manila to building a property portfolio across multiple U.S. states embodies both the promise and challenges of the American Dream. Born and raised in the Philippines, they learned the fundamentals of hustle and business acumen from family—including a grandfather who worked until age 80—before making the life-changing decision to cross the Pacific and start anew in America.

Beginning their American story in Texas, the author has navigated the complex world of real estate investing across several states, including Ohio and Texas. Their investment journey spans from Cleveland discoveries to Dallas gambles, encompassing both significant wins and costly mistakes that provided invaluable education along the way.

Through firsthand experience managing multiple properties, dealing with tax complications, and learning the psychology of both success and failure in real estate, the author has developed a unique perspective on wealth building as an immigrant in America.

Their story is one of resilience, adaptation, and the continuous pursuit of financial independence while honoring their Filipino heritage and family legacy.

Currently managing a diverse real estate portfolio, the author shares their unfiltered experiences—including the failures, misconceptions, and hard-won lessons that traditional real estate education often overlooks. Their work bridges the gap between immigrant ambition and American opportunity, offering practical insights for fellow immigrants and aspiring real estate investors alike.

This book represents their commitment to transparency in sharing both the triumphs and setbacks of building wealth in America, while exploring what it truly means to pursue the American Dream in the 21st century.

www.ingramcontent.com/pod-product-compliance
Lightning Source LLC
Chambersburg PA
CBHW050113170426
43198CB00014B/2563